small dog
BIG UNIVERSE

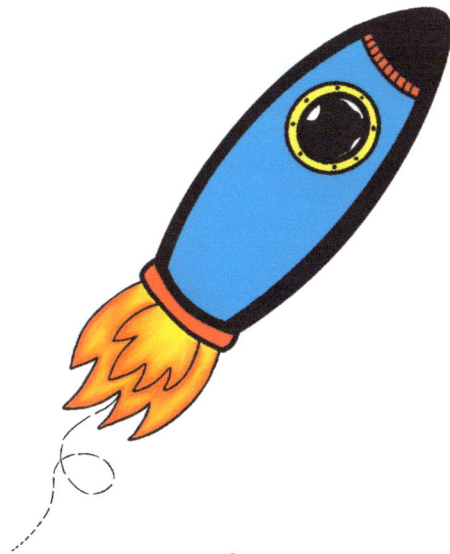

written by
Trista McReynolds

illustrated by
Gentry McReynolds

ISBN 979-8-218-17990-8

Printed in the U.S.A. Published by Loyston Point Press, Tennessee.

First printing, July 2023

Cover and interior typography: Teresa McNelly

To the goodest boy and bestest buddy.

In memory of Frank the Pug
2011-2022

My name is Frank.

I am a dog.

I am small.

This is my family.

It is big.

My family is big but

I am small.

This is my house.

My family lives in a house.

It is big.

My house is big.

My family is small.

My house is in a neighborhood.
It is big.

My neighborhood is big.
My house is small.

My neighborhood is in a city.
It is big.

My city is big.
My neighborhood is small.

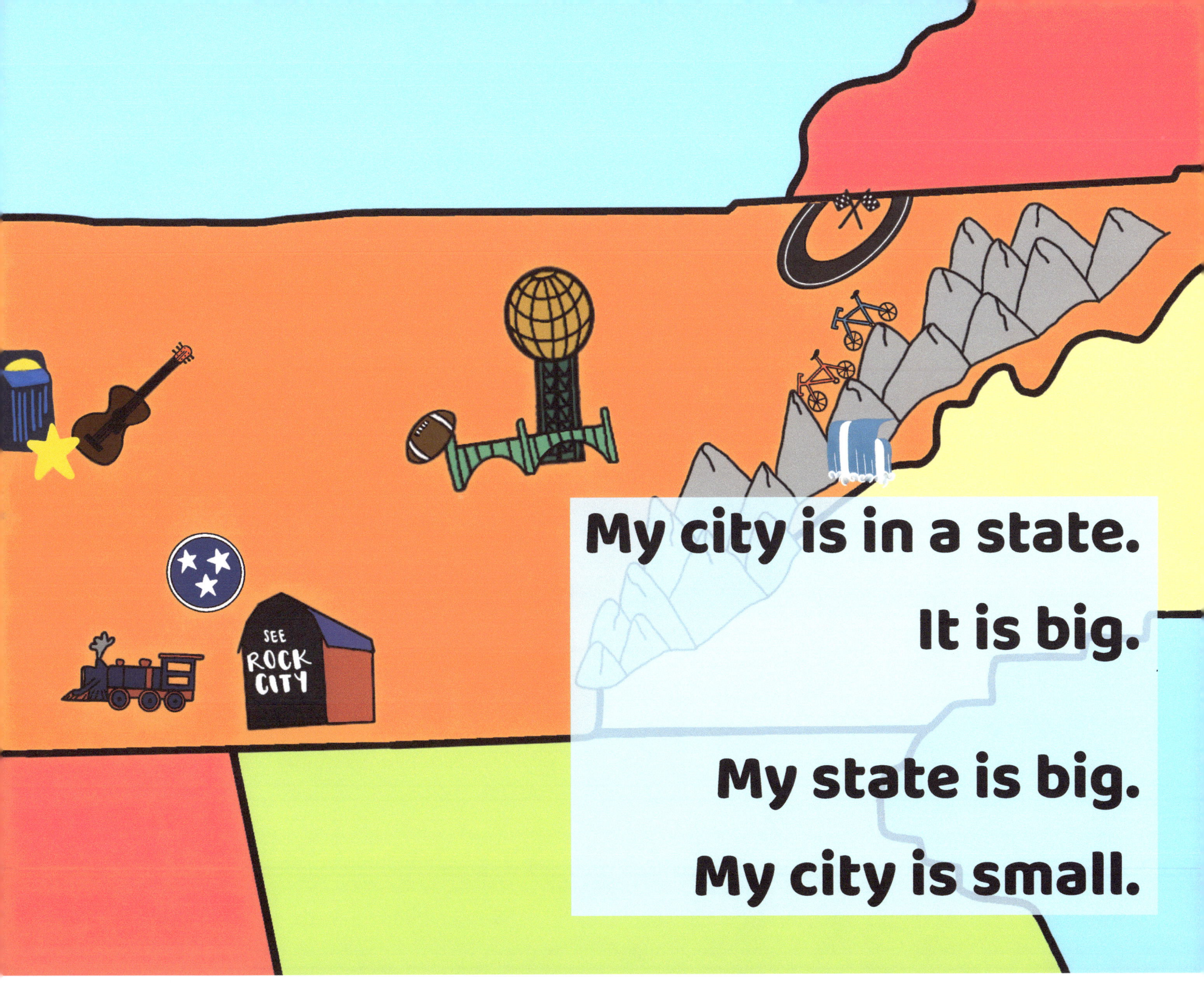

My city is in a state.

It is big.

My state is big.

My city is small.

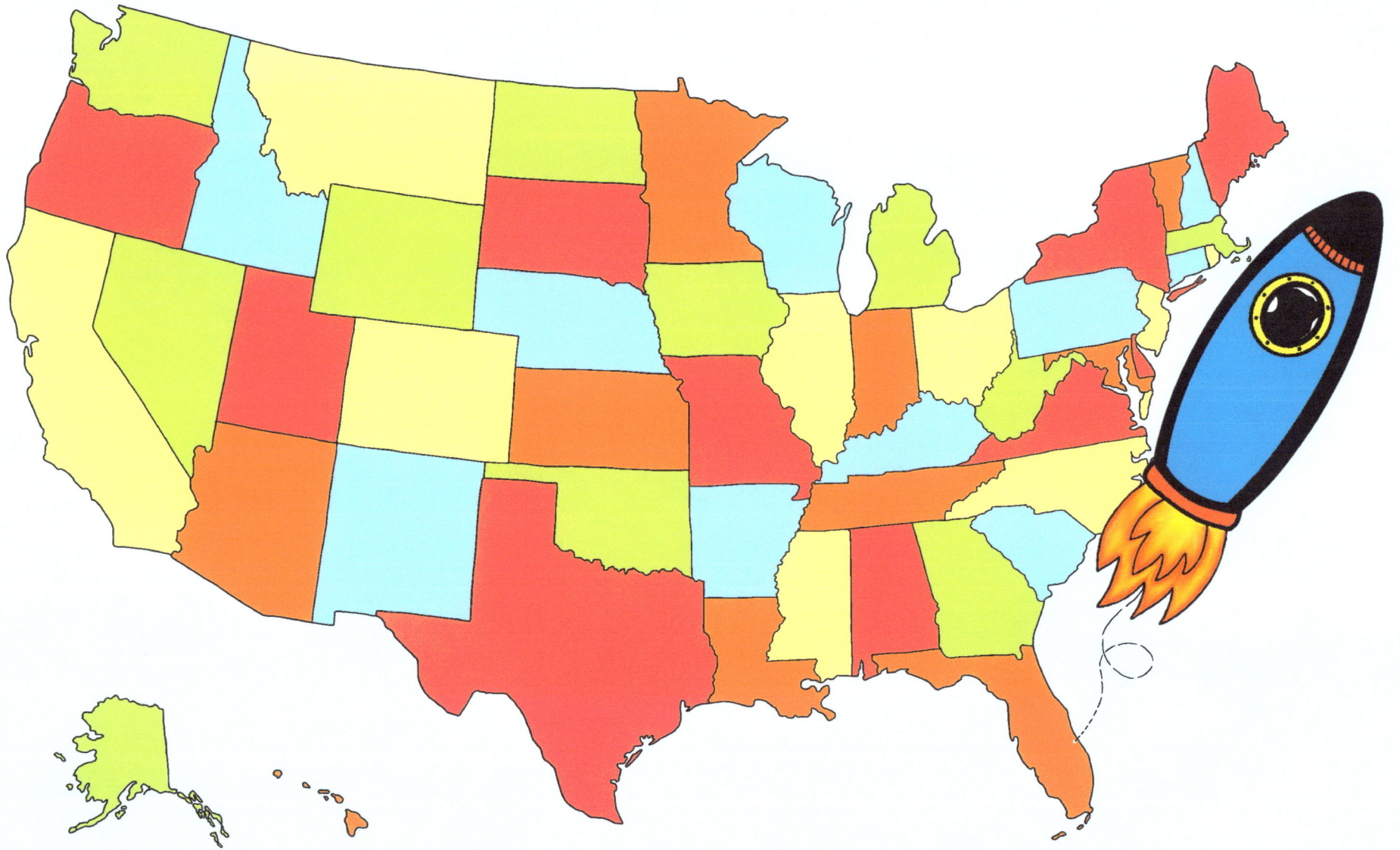

My state is in a country.

It is big.

My country is big.

My state is small.

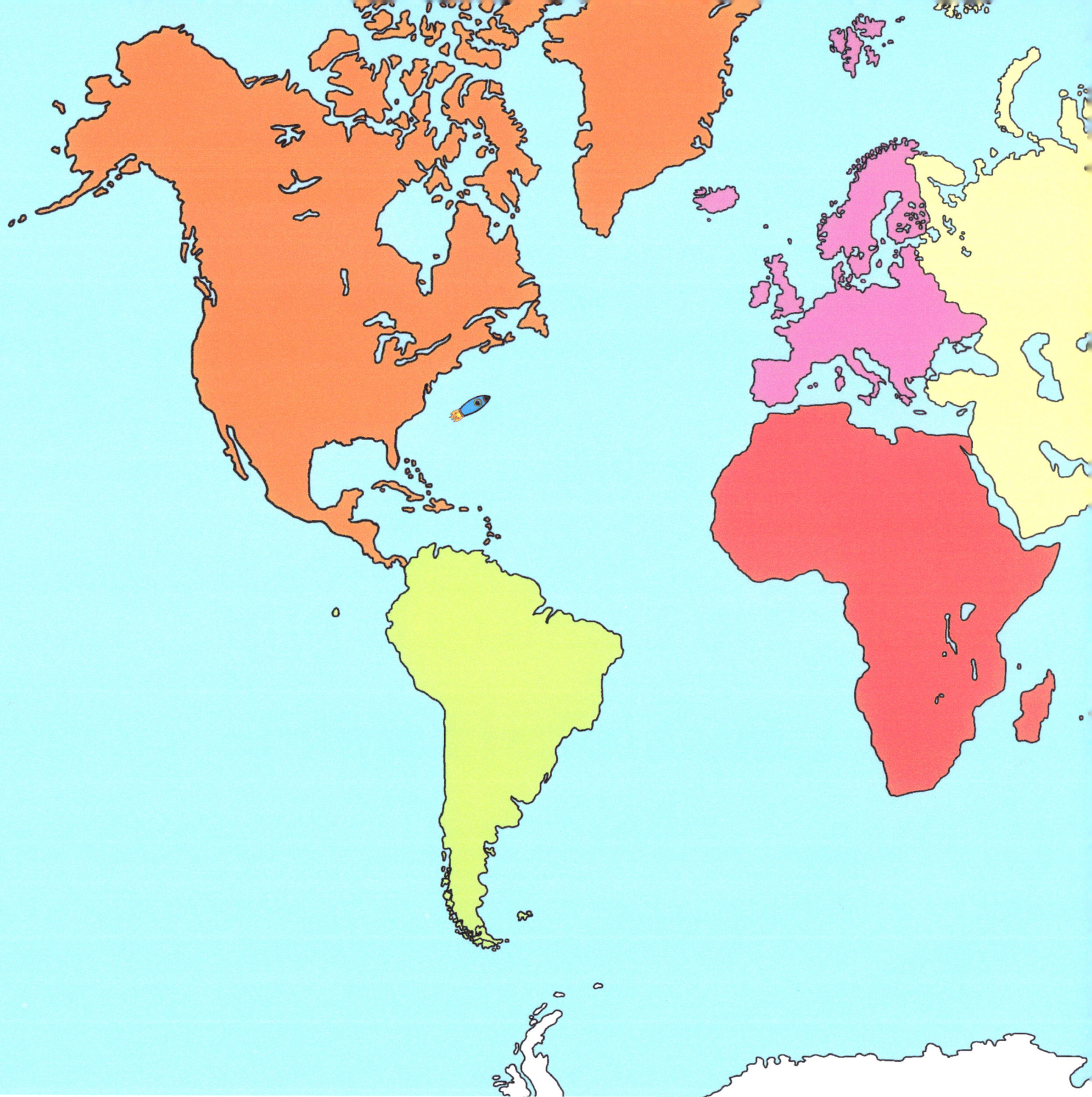

My country is a part of a continent.
It is big.

My continent is big.
My country is small.

My continent is on a planet.
It is big.

My planet is big.
My continent is small.

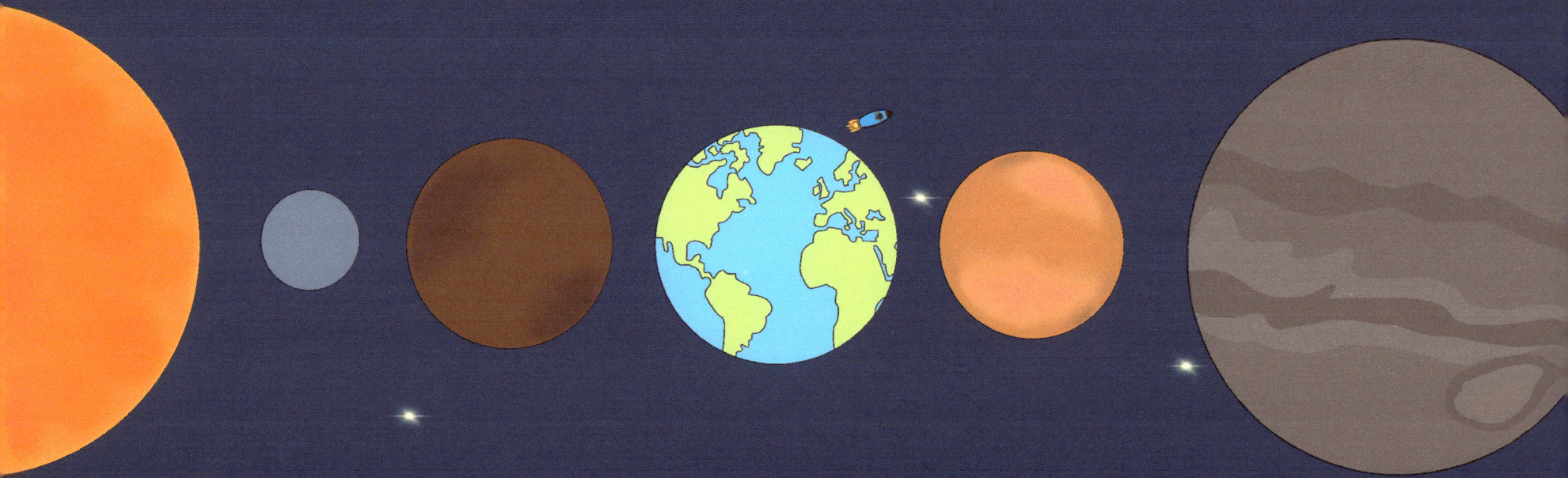

My planet is part of a solar system.
It is big.

My solar system is big.

My planet is small.

My solar system is in a galaxy.
It is big.

My galaxy is big.
My solar system is small.

My galaxy is in the universe.
It is big.

My universe is big.
My galaxy is small.

My universe was made by God.
He is big.

My universe is small.
My God is big.

I am Frank.
I am a dog.
I have a family.
I live in a house
in a neighborhood
in a city
in a state
in a country
on a continent
on a planet
in a solar system
in a galaxy
in a universe...made by God.

Since earliest times men have seen the earth and sky and all God made and have known of His existence and great eternal power. So, they will have no excuse when they stand before God at Judgment Day.
~ Romans 1:20 (TLB) ~

For God loved the world so much that He gave His only Son (Jesus) so that anyone who believes in Him shall not perish but have eternal life.
~ John 3:16 (GNTD) ~

For salvation that comes from trusting Christ is already within easy reach of each of us; in fact, it is as near as our own hearts and mouths. For if you tell others with your own mouth that Jesus Christ is your Lord and believe in your own heart that God has raised him from the dead, you will be saved.
~ Romans 10:8-9 (TLB) ~

Dear Jesus,

I believe you are the Son of God. I believe you came to die for my sins so that we could be together forever. I am sorry for the things I have done wrong. Help me to do right. I give my life to you. I believe and trust in you. Thank you for saving me.